MW01626197

This planner belongs to:

Obedience

in me,

Email us at FREEBIES@JUNELUCY.COM
to get a FREE printable download!

FOR A LITTLE INSPIRATION
follow along at:

@JUNEANDLUCY

@JUNEANDLUCY

WWW.JUNELUCY.COM

Shop our other books at
www.junelucy.com

For questions and customer service, email us at
support@junelucy.com

ISBN 978-1-64608-376-3

The Ultimate FITNESS PLANNER

12 WEEK HEALTH & WELLNESS JOURNAL

Hi my fitness friends!

I'm Sara and I'm so excited for you to dive into this planner. I am a health and wellness coach, mother of three, and lover of coffee. Growing up in Louisiana, I loved my fried food and preferred reading and watching TV over physical activity. If you told me ten years ago that I'd love my veggies and run for fun, I'd have laughed in your face. So let me tell you, if I can do it — so can you!

When my first child was born, a switch flipped in my brain. Here is a daughter that I love beyond my wildest comprehension and I want her to grow up happy, healthy, and confident. I wanted her to love running around, being active, and appreciating nourishing foods. I thought to myself, "If this is what I want for my daughter, then I have to do this too."

My fitness journey was not an easy one! After the birth of two boys, I had three times the meals to cook, rides to chauffeur, and loads of laundry to do. My youngest was born with Down Syndrome at only 25 weeks and with that came an extended hospital stay and lots of doctor and specialist visits in the coming years. Then more than ever I realized how important it was to take care of myself. Squeezing workouts and healthy meals in between visits to the NICU became a lifeline along with the support of my amazing husband and our community. Now our youngest is almost three, and as I was tucking him into bed last night I thought, "WOW. After all those struggles, trials, challenges, highs and lows. We made it. We did it."

Starting my own business built around fitness was a huge leap of faith. Working while being a good partner to my husband and mother to my kids took up the bulk of my day and I soon learned the importance of carving out time to take care of myself. I learned that being a good mother doesn't mean my kids get everything and I get nothing. I'm allowed to take that walk, to work out and not feel guilty, and to enjoy a quiet moment to myself in the morning (latte in hand, preferably).

I have learned to prioritize my physical and nutritional health for my own benefit as well as my loved ones'. One of my favorite tools has been tracking my progress along the way. This is why I am beyond excited about this planner. These pages hold space for you to document both the numbers as well as the non-scale victories. I still remember my first minute-long plank after the birth of my middle son because I wrote it down. It's not just the marathons, the 15-pound weight losses, and the month with no sugar that matter. It's the feeling of getting stronger, of sleeping better, and handling the tough moments life throws at us. And sometimes we need to see those things written on a page to believe them - and more importantly - to celebrate them.

I can't wait for you to get started with this planner and document the highs and lows, the milestone moments and the tiny victories. Hopefully it pushes you, motivates you, and encourages you to fall in love with yourself and the life you are living.

♡Sara

How to use this planner

Start your day from a place of calm instead of chaos by taking a few moments to set your goals and intentions for the day. Jot down what you hope to accomplish today, whether it is work, fitness, nutrition, or personal. Utilize daily affirmations, meditation, and gratitude journaling to put yourself in a positive mindset to start your day with your best foot forward.

activity

15 minutes of morning yoga and stretching

30 minute full-body circuit workout

STEPS: 10,108

Here is where you will document your physical activity for the day. Did you take a killer 50-minute barre class? Walk around the park with a friend? Take a day off to recharge? Write it down! Not every day will include an intense, calorie-busting workout, but strive to move your body in some capacity every single day. Your body will thank you for every HIIT workout, brisk walk, and bike ride you do.

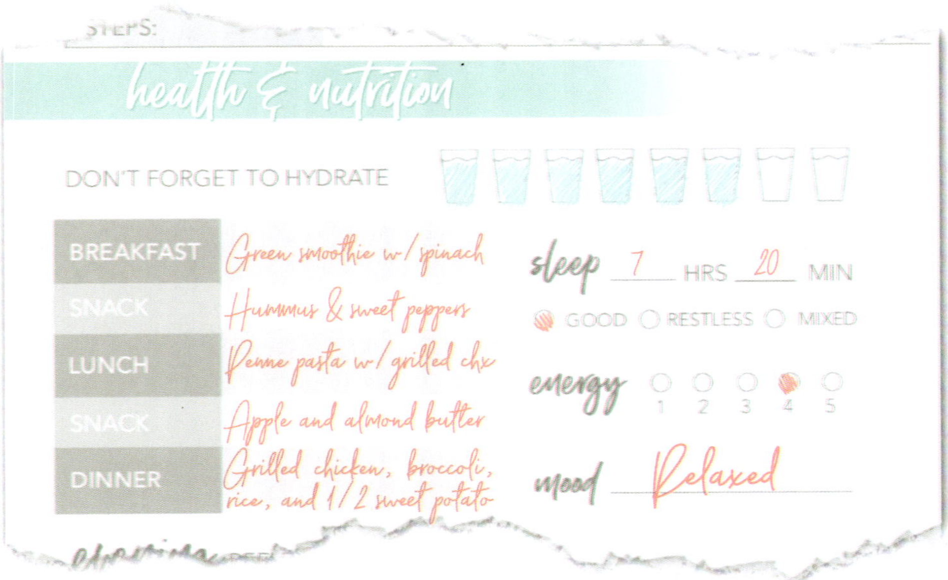

This space will help you track your health and nutrition for the day. Pay close attention to how your physical activity and food intake affect things like sleep quality, mood and energy levels. Did your low energy day coincide with lots of carbs and sugar-laden foods? Are you not eating enough protein at dinner and waking up in the middle of the night? Documenting these behaviors helps set intentional plans and goals going forward.

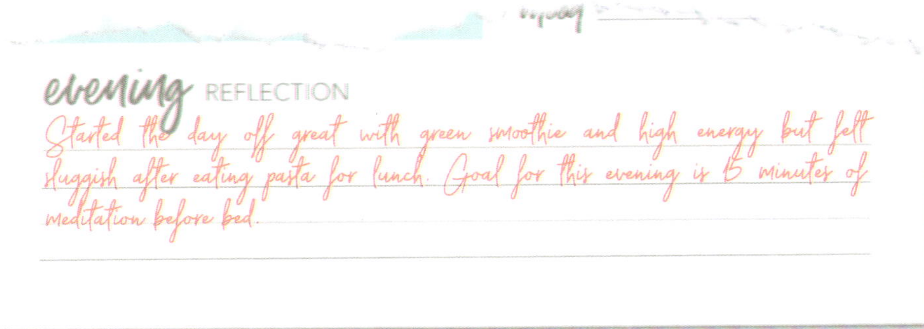

Evening reflections are a great way to process your day in bite-sized chunks. Recap accomplishments you are especially proud of and things you hope to improve upon tomorrow. Try to incorporate gratitude journaling or evening meditations to put yourself in a relaxed mindset and encourage a good night's sleep.

How to use this planner

GOALS:

This planner is set up with goal check-ins every four weeks. At the start of the journal, you will fill out your four-point goal chart. This chart sets forth both the short-term and long-term goals you hope to achieve throughout the next 12 weeks. It can be helpful to try to list out two or three things you need to do in order to meet each goal.

At each subsequent goal check-in, look back to your initial goal chart and determine how much progress you are making. Are you right on track or a little behind? Do you need to reevaluate any of your goals? Do you need to make any adjustments to your workouts, nutrition, or lifestyle in order to meet your goals? Have you already met some of your goals and you want to add some more? Use these goal check-in pages to help you stay on track and make the most out of these 12 weeks!

FITNESS: These will be goals related to your physical activity and your physical fitness. A good, broad goal might be to move your body every day. More personalized goals may be to lose 5 pounds, run 20 minutes without stopping, or add a certain amount of weight to your bicep curls.

NUTRITION: Your nutrition goals should be tailored to your needs. Whether you are keeping a certain calorie limit, reducing sugar, trying to eat less fast food, or upping your veggie intake, be sure to set attainable goals for yourself. At your check-ins, take a look at how your body and mind are responding to your diet and determine if you want to adjust your goals or incorporate additional ones.

LIFESTYLE: You also want to make sure you set some general lifestyle goals for yourself. Maybe you want to set time aside to read four new books, watch less TV, get a jump start on spring cleaning, or start a new hobby. Any personal improvement you've been looking to do should start now and writing them down is the first step to commit to them and make them happen!

WELLNESS: Wellness goals will focus on your mental health and self-care. Here is where you will set goals related to your sleep (whether that be total number of hours a night or a certain time to go to bed and time to rise), increased energy, reducing your anxiety, or maintaining a better mood. Starting a gratitude journal or practicing daily meditation are great wellness goals that contribute to strong mental and emotional health.

REFLECTION:

At each four-week check-in you are also provided a blank page to document your general reflections. Here is where you should note how you are feeling overall, what areas you'd like to see improvement, and what steps you can take to get there. Use this space to celebrate all the number and non-scale victories you have achieved! There is so much more to be proud of than just weight loss. Are you sleeping better or seeing an improvement in your mood? Do you feel better when you work out in the morning versus the evening? What foods are you having trouble with? Write down any compliments you have received that made you feel good about yourself. You can also use this space to recap and reassess your fitness journey because you have made so much progress and you should be proud!

Measurements 101

Tips for taking accurate and consistent measurements

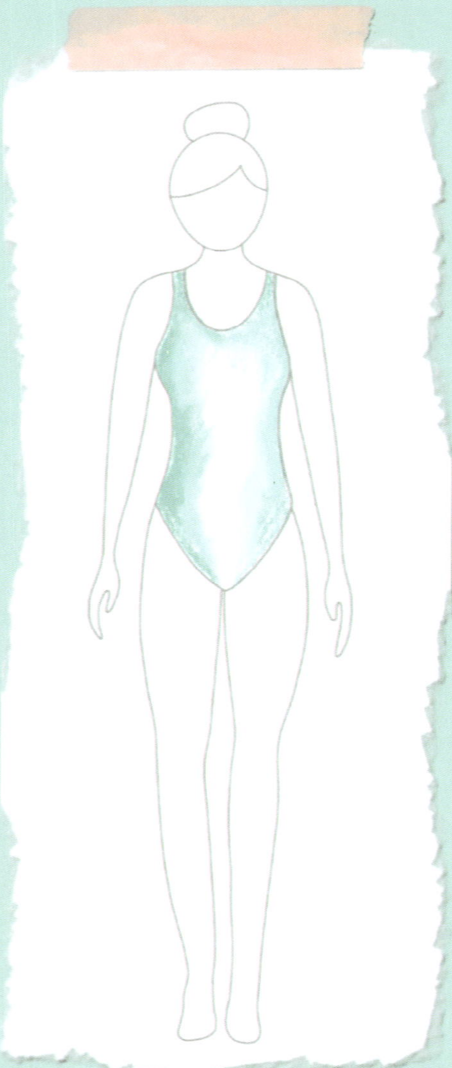

When we talk about non-scale victories, one of the best ways to see improvement in physical fitness is by measuring our bodies. As we get stronger and our stamina increases, we see changes in our body that are not necessarily reflected in our weight. All you need to take your measurements is a measuring tape. There are five key measurements that you'll want to keep track of during your fitness journey:

ARMS: place your right thumb on your left shoulder and stretch your pinky down toward the center of your bicep. Where your pinky lands is where you should measure around your arm.

CHEST: bring the measuring tape around you behind your back and measure across your chest at the nipple line. Make sure your elbows are down by your side and not sticking out.

WAIST: bring the measuring tape behind your back and measure across using your belly button as the center point.

HIPS: bring your feet together and measure around the widest part of your hips.

LEGS: place your pinky on your knee and stretch your thumb up toward your thigh. Where your thumb lands is the center point of your leg you should measure.

Many people like to track their progress by taking photos before, during, and at the end of a fitness challenge. For best results, take your photos in front of a plain background, like a door or wall. Consistency is key so make sure to take your pictures in the same location wearing the same outfit each time.

goal digger

Your goals should always be SMART, that is:

Specific Don't be overly broad. Instead of "lose weight" try "lose 3 pounds."

Measurable Make sure you are able to prove that you are making progress, so instead of "build up my endurance" try "run 2 miles without stopping."

Attainable Your goals should be realistic and should align with your long-term objectives. Setting goals that are not realistic in the time period you are working in will only make you feel defeated rather than help you celebrate the huge progress you ARE making.

Relevant Make sure your short term goals align with your long-term objectives!

Time-Based Set a realistic target date so that you can prioritize and stay motivated! Twelve weeks is a great time period for setting goals since it is long enough to make an impact but short enough to stay on track.

let's do this.

FITNESS

NUTRITION

LIFESTYLE

WELLNESS

Measurements

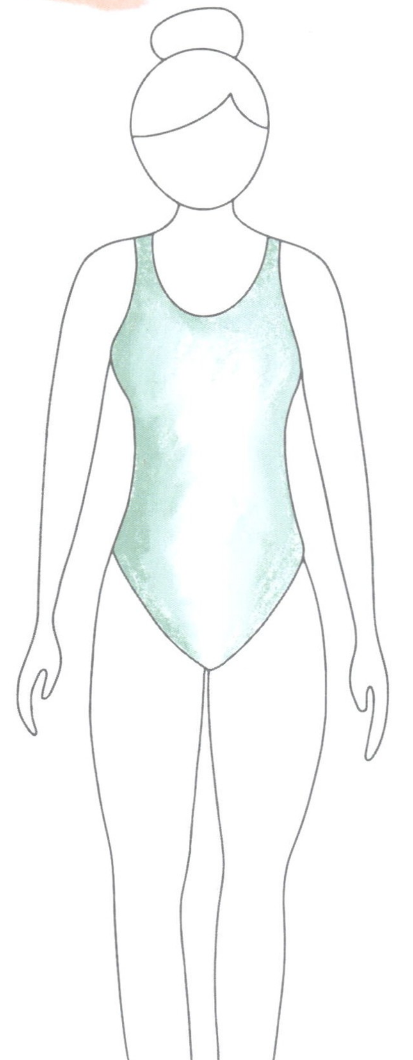

DATE: ______________________

UPPER ARM:

LEFT: ______________________

RIGHT: ______________________

CHEST: ______________________

WAIST: ______________________

HIPS: ______________________

LEGS:

LEFT: ______________________

RIGHT: ______________________

WEIGHT: ______________________

See page 10 for tips on getting accurate and consistent measurements!

One huge hurdle we all have to contend with at the beginning of a fitness journey is starting from square one. The mountain ahead looks a heck of a lot bigger when you're standing at the base than when you've climbed a bit. But we can't compare our Day 1 to someone else's Day 500. You have to start where you are and use what you have. If it takes jogging in 20 second spurts or practicing planks against the wall to get you going, then embrace the journey. The key is to do it consistently. When we start out, it may take some self-negotiating every single day to put on the workout clothes and move our body. But after some time passes, fitness and health become second nature and we can't imagine not incorporating exercise and healthy eating into our day. Good habits start with small, consistent building blocks.

Motivation is what gets you started.

Habit is what keeps you going.

DATE: ____________ M T W Th F S S

morning GOALS & INTENTIONS

activity

STEPS:

health & nutrition

DON'T FORGET TO HYDRATE

BREAKFAST	
SNACK	
LUNCH	
SNACK	
DINNER	

sleep ______ HRS ______ MIN

○ GOOD ○ RESTLESS ○ MIXED

energy ○ 1 ○ 2 ○ 3 ○ 4 ○ 5

mood ____________

evening REFLECTION

DATE: ____________ M T W Th F S S

morning GOALS & INTENTIONS

activity

STEPS:

health & nutrition

DON'T FORGET TO HYDRATE

BREAKFAST	
SNACK	
LUNCH	
SNACK	
DINNER	

sleep ______ HRS ______ MIN

○ GOOD ○ RESTLESS ○ MIXED

energy ○ 1 ○ 2 ○ 3 ○ 4 ○ 5

mood ____________

evening REFLECTION

DATE: ______________________ M T W Th F S S

morning GOALS & INTENTIONS

activity

STEPS:

health & nutrition

DON'T FORGET TO HYDRATE

BREAKFAST	
SNACK	
LUNCH	
SNACK	
DINNER	

sleep ________ HRS ________ MIN

○ GOOD ○ RESTLESS ○ MIXED

energy ○ 1 ○ 2 ○ 3 ○ 4 ○ 5

mood ______________________

evening REFLECTION

DATE: ______________ M T W Th F S S

morning GOALS & INTENTIONS

activity

STEPS:

health & nutrition

DON'T FORGET TO HYDRATE

BREAKFAST	
SNACK	
LUNCH	
SNACK	
DINNER	

sleep ______ HRS ______ MIN

○ GOOD ○ RESTLESS ○ MIXED

energy ○ 1 ○ 2 ○ 3 ○ 4 ○ 5

mood ______________

evening REFLECTION

DATE: ____________ M T W Th F S S

morning GOALS & INTENTIONS

activity

STEPS:

health & nutrition

DON'T FORGET TO HYDRATE

BREAKFAST	
SNACK	
LUNCH	
SNACK	
DINNER	

sleep ______ HRS ______ MIN

○ GOOD ○ RESTLESS ○ MIXED

energy ○ 1 ○ 2 ○ 3 ○ 4 ○ 5

mood ____________

evening REFLECTION

The one wellness tip that EVERYONE needs to hear:

hydrate hydrate hydrate!

From clear skin to extra energy, water is a magical elixir that provides unending value to your body. But how can a person drink water when coffee and wine exist? Flavor your water with a squeeze of lemon or sliced strawberries. Buy a cute water jug and carry it everywhere. Have a "water buddy" and text each other fun emojis when you reach your water goal for the day. Do what you need to do to ensure you are drinking half your body weight in ounces every day. Your body will thank you for it!

DATE: ______________ M T W Th F S S

morning GOALS & INTENTIONS

activity

STEPS:

health & nutrition

DON'T FORGET TO HYDRATE

BREAKFAST	
SNACK	
LUNCH	
SNACK	
DINNER	

sleep ______ HRS ______ MIN

○ GOOD ○ RESTLESS ○ MIXED

energy ○ 1 ○ 2 ○ 3 ○ 4 ○ 5

mood ______________

evening REFLECTION

DATE: ______________________ M T W Th F S S

morning GOALS & INTENTIONS

activity

STEPS:

health & nutrition

DON'T FORGET TO HYDRATE

BREAKFAST	
SNACK	
LUNCH	
SNACK	
DINNER	

sleep ________ HRS ________ MIN

○ GOOD ○ RESTLESS ○ MIXED

energy ○ 1 ○ 2 ○ 3 ○ 4 ○ 5

mood ______________________

evening REFLECTION

DATE: ____________________ M T W Th F S S

morning GOALS & INTENTIONS

activity

STEPS:

health & nutrition

DON'T FORGET TO HYDRATE

BREAKFAST	
SNACK	
LUNCH	
SNACK	
DINNER	

sleep ______ HRS ______ MIN

○ GOOD ○ RESTLESS ○ MIXED

energy ○ 1 ○ 2 ○ 3 ○ 4 ○ 5

mood ____________________

evening REFLECTION

DATE: ____________________ M T W Th F S S

morning GOALS & INTENTIONS

activity

STEPS:

health & nutrition

DON'T FORGET TO HYDRATE

BREAKFAST	
SNACK	
LUNCH	
SNACK	
DINNER	

sleep ______ HRS ______ MIN

○ GOOD ○ RESTLESS ○ MIXED

energy ○ 1 ○ 2 ○ 3 ○ 4 ○ 5

mood ____________________

evening REFLECTION

DATE: ______________________ M T W Th F S S

morning GOALS & INTENTIONS

activity

STEPS:

health & nutrition

DON'T FORGET TO HYDRATE

BREAKFAST	
SNACK	
LUNCH	
SNACK	
DINNER	

sleep ________ HRS ________ MIN

○ GOOD ○ RESTLESS ○ MIXED

energy ○ 1 ○ 2 ○ 3 ○ 4 ○ 5

mood ____________________

evening REFLECTION

DATE: ____________________ M T W Th F S S

morning GOALS & INTENTIONS

activity

STEPS:

health & nutrition

DON'T FORGET TO HYDRATE

BREAKFAST	
SNACK	
LUNCH	
SNACK	
DINNER	

sleep ______ HRS ______ MIN

○ GOOD ○ RESTLESS ○ MIXED

energy ○ 1 ○ 2 ○ 3 ○ 4 ○ 5

mood ____________________

evening REFLECTION

DATE: ______________ M T W Th F S S

morning GOALS & INTENTIONS

activity

STEPS:

health & nutrition

DON'T FORGET TO HYDRATE

BREAKFAST	
SNACK	
LUNCH	
SNACK	
DINNER	

sleep ______ HRS ______ MIN

○ GOOD ○ RESTLESS ○ MIXED

energy ○ 1 ○ 2 ○ 3 ○ 4 ○ 5

mood ______

evening REFLECTION

DATE: ____________ M T W Th F S S

morning GOALS & INTENTIONS

activity

STEPS:

health & nutrition

DON'T FORGET TO HYDRATE

BREAKFAST	
SNACK	
LUNCH	
SNACK	
DINNER	

sleep ______ HRS ______ MIN

○ GOOD ○ RESTLESS ○ MIXED

energy ○ 1 ○ 2 ○ 3 ○ 4 ○ 5

mood ____________

evening REFLECTION

DATE: ______________ M T W Th F S S

morning GOALS & INTENTIONS

activity

STEPS:

health & nutrition

DON'T FORGET TO HYDRATE

BREAKFAST

SNACK

LUNCH

SNACK

DINNER

sleep ______ HRS ______ MIN

○ GOOD ○ RESTLESS ○ MIXED

energy ○ 1 ○ 2 ○ 3 ○ 4 ○ 5

mood ______________

evening REFLECTION

DATE: ______________________ M T W Th F S S

morning GOALS & INTENTIONS

activity

STEPS:

health & nutrition

DON'T FORGET TO HYDRATE

BREAKFAST

SNACK

LUNCH

SNACK

DINNER

sleep ______ HRS ______ MIN

○ GOOD ○ RESTLESS ○ MIXED

energy ○ 1 ○ 2 ○ 3 ○ 4 ○ 5

mood ______________________

evening REFLECTION

DATE: ______________ M T W Th F S S

morning GOALS & INTENTIONS

activity

STEPS:

health & nutrition

DON'T FORGET TO HYDRATE

BREAKFAST	
SNACK	
LUNCH	
SNACK	
DINNER	

sleep ______ HRS ______ MIN

○ GOOD ○ RESTLESS ○ MIXED

energy ○ 1 ○ 2 ○ 3 ○ 4 ○ 5

mood ______________

evening REFLECTION

DATE: ____________ M T W Th F S S

morning GOALS & INTENTIONS

activity

STEPS:

health & nutrition

DON'T FORGET TO HYDRATE

BREAKFAST	
SNACK	
LUNCH	
SNACK	
DINNER	

sleep ______ HRS ______ MIN

○ GOOD ○ RESTLESS ○ MIXED

energy ○ 1 ○ 2 ○ 3 ○ 4 ○ 5

mood ______________

evening REFLECTION

DATE: ______________________ M T W Th F S S

morning GOALS & INTENTIONS

activity

STEPS:

health & nutrition

DON'T FORGET TO HYDRATE

BREAKFAST	
SNACK	
LUNCH	
SNACK	
DINNER	

sleep ______ HRS ______ MIN

○ GOOD ○ RESTLESS ○ MIXED

energy ○ 1 ○ 2 ○ 3 ○ 4 ○ 5

mood ______________

evening REFLECTION

DATE: ______________________. M T W Th F S S

morning GOALS & INTENTIONS

activity

STEPS:

health & nutrition

DON'T FORGET TO HYDRATE

BREAKFAST	
SNACK	
LUNCH	
SNACK	
DINNER	

sleep ________ HRS ________ MIN

○ GOOD ○ RESTLESS ○ MIXED

energy ○ 1 ○ 2 ○ 3 ○ 4 ○ 5

mood ____________________

evening REFLECTION

DATE: ______________ M T W Th F S S

morning GOALS & INTENTIONS

____

____

____

____

activity

STEPS:

health & nutrition

DON'T FORGET TO HYDRATE

BREAKFAST	
SNACK	
LUNCH	
SNACK	
DINNER	

sleep ______ HRS ______ MIN

○ GOOD ○ RESTLESS ○ MIXED

energy ○ 1 ○ 2 ○ 3 ○ 4 ○ 5

mood ______________

evening REFLECTION

____

____

____

____

if
not
now
then
when?

DATE: ____________________ M T W Th F S S

morning GOALS & INTENTIONS

activity

STEPS:

health & nutrition

DON'T FORGET TO HYDRATE

BREAKFAST	
SNACK	
LUNCH	
SNACK	
DINNER	

sleep ______ HRS ______ MIN

○ GOOD ○ RESTLESS ○ MIXED

energy ○ 1 ○ 2 ○ 3 ○ 4 ○ 5

mood ____________

evening REFLECTION

DATE: ____________ M T W Th F S S

morning GOALS & INTENTIONS

activity

STEPS:

health & nutrition

DON'T FORGET TO HYDRATE

BREAKFAST	
SNACK	
LUNCH	
SNACK	
DINNER	

sleep ______ HRS ______ MIN

○ GOOD ○ RESTLESS ○ MIXED

energy ○ 1 ○ 2 ○ 3 ○ 4 ○ 5

mood ____________

evening REFLECTION

DATE: ____________ M T W Th F S S

morning GOALS & INTENTIONS

activity

STEPS:

health & nutrition

DON'T FORGET TO HYDRATE

BREAKFAST	
SNACK	
LUNCH	
SNACK	
DINNER	

sleep ______ HRS ______ MIN

○ GOOD ○ RESTLESS ○ MIXED

energy ○ 1 ○ 2 ○ 3 ○ 4 ○ 5

mood ____________

evening REFLECTION

DATE: ____________________ M T W Th F S S

morning GOALS & INTENTIONS

activity

STEPS:

health & nutrition

DON'T FORGET TO HYDRATE

BREAKFAST	
SNACK	
LUNCH	
SNACK	
DINNER	

sleep ______ HRS ______ MIN

○ GOOD ○ RESTLESS ○ MIXED

energy ○ 1 ○ 2 ○ 3 ○ 4 ○ 5

mood ____________________

evening REFLECTION

DATE: ____________ M T W Th F S S

morning GOALS & INTENTIONS

activity

STEPS:

health & nutrition

DON'T FORGET TO HYDRATE

BREAKFAST	
SNACK	
LUNCH	
SNACK	
DINNER	

sleep ______ HRS ______ MIN

○ GOOD ○ RESTLESS ○ MIXED

energy ○ 1 ○ 2 ○ 3 ○ 4 ○ 5

mood ____________

evening REFLECTION

DATE: ______________ M T W Th F S S

morning GOALS & INTENTIONS

activity

STEPS:

health & nutrition

DON'T FORGET TO HYDRATE

BREAKFAST	
SNACK	
LUNCH	
SNACK	
DINNER	

sleep ______ HRS ______ MIN

○ GOOD ○ RESTLESS ○ MIXED

energy ○ 1 ○ 2 ○ 3 ○ 4 ○ 5

mood ______________

evening REFLECTION

DATE: ____________________ M T W Th F S S

morning GOALS & INTENTIONS

activity

STEPS:

health & nutrition

DON'T FORGET TO HYDRATE

BREAKFAST	
SNACK	
LUNCH	
SNACK	
DINNER	

sleep ______ HRS ______ MIN

○ GOOD ○ RESTLESS ○ MIXED

energy ○ 1 ○ 2 ○ 3 ○ 4 ○ 5

mood ____________

evening REFLECTION

You may
not be
there yet,
but you're
closer than
you were
yesterday.

Measurements

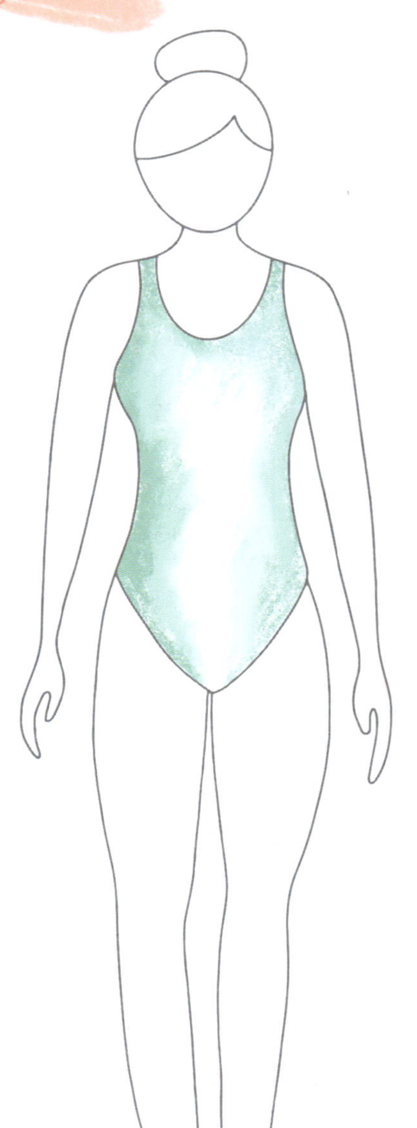

DATE: ____________________

UPPER ARM:

LEFT: ____________________

RIGHT: ____________________

CHEST: ____________________

WAIST: ____________________

HIPS: ____________________

LEGS:

LEFT: ____________________

RIGHT: ____________________

WEIGHT: ____________________

See page 10 for tips on getting accurate and consistent measurements!

Check-in time!

FITNESS

NUTRITION

GOALS

LIFESTYLE

WELLNESS

Reflection

DATE: ______________ M T W Th F S S

morning GOALS & INTENTIONS

activity

STEPS:

health & nutrition

DON'T FORGET TO HYDRATE

BREAKFAST	
SNACK	
LUNCH	
SNACK	
DINNER	

sleep ______ HRS ______ MIN

○ GOOD ○ RESTLESS ○ MIXED

energy ○ 1 ○ 2 ○ 3 ○ 4 ○ 5

mood ______________

evening REFLECTION

DATE: ____________________ M T W Th F S S

morning GOALS & INTENTIONS

activity

STEPS:

health & nutrition

DON'T FORGET TO HYDRATE

BREAKFAST	
SNACK	
LUNCH	
SNACK	
DINNER	

sleep ______ HRS ______ MIN

○ GOOD ○ RESTLESS ○ MIXED

energy ○ 1 ○ 2 ○ 3 ○ 4 ○ 5

mood ____________________

evening REFLECTION

DATE: ________________ M T W Th F S S

morning GOALS & INTENTIONS

activity

STEPS:

health & nutrition

DON'T FORGET TO HYDRATE

BREAKFAST	
SNACK	
LUNCH	
SNACK	
DINNER	

sleep ______ HRS ______ MIN

○ GOOD ○ RESTLESS ○ MIXED

energy ○ 1 ○ 2 ○ 3 ○ 4 ○ 5

mood ______________

evening REFLECTION

DATE: ______________ M T W Th F S S

morning GOALS & INTENTIONS

activity

STEPS:

health & nutrition

DON'T FORGET TO HYDRATE

BREAKFAST	
SNACK	
LUNCH	
SNACK	
DINNER	

sleep ______ HRS ______ MIN

○ GOOD ○ RESTLESS ○ MIXED

energy ○ 1 ○ 2 ○ 3 ○ 4 ○ 5

mood ______________

evening REFLECTION

DATE: ________________ M T W Th F S S

morning GOALS & INTENTIONS

activity

STEPS:

health & nutrition

DON'T FORGET TO HYDRATE

BREAKFAST	
SNACK	
LUNCH	
SNACK	
DINNER	

sleep ______ HRS ______ MIN

○ GOOD ○ RESTLESS ○ MIXED

energy ○ 1 ○ 2 ○ 3 ○ 4 ○ 5

mood ________________

evening REFLECTION

DATE: ______________________ M T W Th F S S

morning GOALS & INTENTIONS

activity

STEPS:

health & nutrition

DON'T FORGET TO HYDRATE

BREAKFAST	
SNACK	
LUNCH	
SNACK	
DINNER	

sleep ________ HRS ________ MIN

○ GOOD ○ RESTLESS ○ MIXED

energy ○ 1 ○ 2 ○ 3 ○ 4 ○ 5

mood ______________________

evening REFLECTION

DATE: ______________________ M T W Th F S S

morning GOALS & INTENTIONS

activity

STEPS:

health & nutrition

DON'T FORGET TO HYDRATE

BREAKFAST	
SNACK	
LUNCH	
SNACK	
DINNER	

sleep ______ HRS ______ MIN

○ GOOD ○ RESTLESS ○ MIXED

energy ○ 1 ○ 2 ○ 3 ○ 4 ○ 5

mood ______________________

evening REFLECTION

Unfortunately for many of us, we have a little voice in our head that constantly criticizes. Negative self-talk is one of the most difficult concepts to overcome for many. This keeps us down and makes it harder to achieve our goals. Work each day to be gentler and kinder to yourself. The next time you think something negative about yourself ask the question, "How would I feel if I heard my daughter/best friend/brother say that to themselves?" Then, replace that negative thought with a positive one. Instead of "I can't even do one pushup" think "How cool that I am working to get stronger!"

When life is especially tough, focus on finding joy in even the smallest things. Change your thinking from everything is happening TO me to what is happening FOR me. Keep a list of things you love about yourself and your life. When that little voice in your head starts to chirp that you're not good enough, read the list aloud to yourself and remind yourself that you are amazing.

DATE: ____________________ M T W Th F S S

morning GOALS & INTENTIONS

___

___

___

___

activity

STEPS:

health & nutrition

DON'T FORGET TO HYDRATE

BREAKFAST	
SNACK	
LUNCH	
SNACK	
DINNER	

sleep ______ HRS ______ MIN

○ GOOD ○ RESTLESS ○ MIXED

energy ○ 1 ○ 2 ○ 3 ○ 4 ○ 5

mood ____________________

evening REFLECTION

___

___

___

___

DATE: ____________________ M T W Th F S S

morning GOALS & INTENTIONS

activity

STEPS:

health & nutrition

DON'T FORGET TO HYDRATE

BREAKFAST	
SNACK	
LUNCH	
SNACK	
DINNER	

sleep ______ HRS ______ MIN

○ GOOD ○ RESTLESS ○ MIXED

energy ○ 1 ○ 2 ○ 3 ○ 4 ○ 5

mood ____________________

evening REFLECTION

DATE: ____________________ M T W Th F S S

morning GOALS & INTENTIONS

____

____

____

____

activity

STEPS:

health & nutrition

DON'T FORGET TO HYDRATE

BREAKFAST	
SNACK	
LUNCH	
SNACK	
DINNER	

sleep ________ HRS ________ MIN

○ GOOD ○ RESTLESS ○ MIXED

energy ○ 1 ○ 2 ○ 3 ○ 4 ○ 5

mood ____________________

evening REFLECTION

____

____

____

____

DATE: ____________________ M T W Th F S S

morning GOALS & INTENTIONS

activity

STEPS:

health & nutrition

DON'T FORGET TO HYDRATE

BREAKFAST	
SNACK	
LUNCH	
SNACK	
DINNER	

sleep ______ HRS ______ MIN

○ GOOD ○ RESTLESS ○ MIXED

energy ○ 1 ○ 2 ○ 3 ○ 4 ○ 5

mood ____________

evening REFLECTION

DATE: ______________ M T W Th F S S

morning GOALS & INTENTIONS

activity

STEPS:

health & nutrition

DON'T FORGET TO HYDRATE

BREAKFAST	
SNACK	
LUNCH	
SNACK	
DINNER	

sleep ______ HRS ______ MIN

○ GOOD ○ RESTLESS ○ MIXED

energy ○ 1 ○ 2 ○ 3 ○ 4 ○ 5

mood ______________

evening REFLECTION

DATE: ______________ M T W Th F S S

morning GOALS & INTENTIONS

activity

STEPS:

health & nutrition

DON'T FORGET TO HYDRATE

BREAKFAST	
SNACK	
LUNCH	
SNACK	
DINNER	

sleep ______ HRS ______ MIN

○ GOOD ○ RESTLESS ○ MIXED

energy ○ 1 ○ 2 ○ 3 ○ 4 ○ 5

mood ______

evening REFLECTION

DATE: ______________ M T W Th F S S

morning GOALS & INTENTIONS

activity

STEPS:

health & nutrition

DON'T FORGET TO HYDRATE

BREAKFAST	
SNACK	
LUNCH	
SNACK	
DINNER	

sleep ______ HRS ______ MIN

○ GOOD ○ RESTLESS ○ MIXED

energy ○ 1 ○ 2 ○ 3 ○ 4 ○ 5

mood ______________

evening REFLECTION

the
best
things in life
aren't instant.
good
things
take time to
grow.

DATE: ____________ M T W Th F S S

morning GOALS & INTENTIONS

activity

STEPS:

health & nutrition

DON'T FORGET TO HYDRATE

BREAKFAST

SNACK

LUNCH

SNACK

DINNER

sleep ______ HRS ______ MIN

○ GOOD ○ RESTLESS ○ MIXED

energy ○ 1 ○ 2 ○ 3 ○ 4 ○ 5

mood ______

evening REFLECTION

DATE: ______________ M T W Th F S S

morning GOALS & INTENTIONS

activity

STEPS:

health & nutrition

DON'T FORGET TO HYDRATE

BREAKFAST	
SNACK	
LUNCH	
SNACK	
DINNER	

sleep ______ HRS ______ MIN

○ GOOD ○ RESTLESS ○ MIXED

energy ○ 1 ○ 2 ○ 3 ○ 4 ○ 5

mood ______________

evening REFLECTION

DATE: ____________ M T W Th F S S

morning GOALS & INTENTIONS

activity

STEPS:

health & nutrition

DON'T FORGET TO HYDRATE

BREAKFAST	
SNACK	
LUNCH	
SNACK	
DINNER	

sleep ______ HRS ______ MIN

○ GOOD ○ RESTLESS ○ MIXED

energy ○ 1 ○ 2 ○ 3 ○ 4 ○ 5

mood ____________

evening REFLECTION

DATE: ____________________ M T W Th F S S

morning GOALS & INTENTIONS

____

____

____

____

activity

STEPS:

health & nutrition

DON'T FORGET TO HYDRATE

BREAKFAST	
SNACK	
LUNCH	
SNACK	
DINNER	

sleep ______ HRS ______ MIN

○ GOOD ○ RESTLESS ○ MIXED

energy ○ 1 ○ 2 ○ 3 ○ 4 ○ 5

mood ______________________

evening REFLECTION

____

____

____

 ____

DATE: ______________________ M T W Th F S S

morning GOALS & INTENTIONS

activity

STEPS:

health & nutrition

DON'T FORGET TO HYDRATE

BREAKFAST	
SNACK	
LUNCH	
SNACK	
DINNER	

sleep ________ HRS ________ MIN

○ GOOD ○ RESTLESS ○ MIXED

energy ○ 1 ○ 2 ○ 3 ○ 4 ○ 5

mood ____________________

evening REFLECTION

DATE: ____________ M T W Th F S S

morning GOALS & INTENTIONS

activity

STEPS:

health & nutrition

DON'T FORGET TO HYDRATE

BREAKFAST	
SNACK	
LUNCH	
SNACK	
DINNER	

sleep ______ HRS ______ MIN

○ GOOD ○ RESTLESS ○ MIXED

energy ○ 1 ○ 2 ○ 3 ○ 4 ○ 5

mood ____________

evening REFLECTION

DATE: ______________ M T W Th F S S

morning GOALS & INTENTIONS

activity

STEPS:

health & nutrition

DON'T FORGET TO HYDRATE

BREAKFAST	
SNACK	
LUNCH	
SNACK	
DINNER	

sleep ______ HRS ______ MIN

○ GOOD ○ RESTLESS ○ MIXED

energy ○ 1 ○ 2 ○ 3 ○ 4 ○ 5

mood ______________

evening REFLECTION

Celebrate the Non-Scale Victories

It is human nature to gauge fitness progress based on the number on the scale. But number of pounds lost is only one small piece of the puzzle and can lead to frustration and regression. Remember to celebrate the non-scale victories too as you continue down your fitness journey.

Are your pants fitting a little looser than they were a month ago?

Did you get a nice compliment from a friend?

Maybe you've noticed you are sleeping better or have less anxiety.

Eating well and being active have so many benefits beyond simply what you weigh. And if you wait until the big goals are completed, you may be left feeling unmotivated or underwhelmed. So celebrate the small victories every day, and you might quickly realize those small victories are sometimes bigger than you think.

DATE: ______________ M T W Th F S S

morning GOALS & INTENTIONS

activity

STEPS:

health & nutrition

DON'T FORGET TO HYDRATE

BREAKFAST	
SNACK	
LUNCH	
SNACK	
DINNER	

sleep ______ HRS ______ MIN

○ GOOD ○ RESTLESS ○ MIXED

energy ○ 1 ○ 2 ○ 3 ○ 4 ○ 5

mood ______________

evening REFLECTION

DATE: ____________________ M T W Th F S S

morning GOALS & INTENTIONS

activity

STEPS:

health & nutrition

DON'T FORGET TO HYDRATE

BREAKFAST	
SNACK	
LUNCH	
SNACK	
DINNER	

sleep ______ HRS ______ MIN

○ GOOD ○ RESTLESS ○ MIXED

energy ○ 1 ○ 2 ○ 3 ○ 4 ○ 5

mood ____________________

evening REFLECTION

DATE: ______________________ M T W Th F S S

morning GOALS & INTENTIONS

activity

STEPS:

health & nutrition

DON'T FORGET TO HYDRATE

BREAKFAST	
SNACK	
LUNCH	
SNACK	
DINNER	

sleep ______ HRS ______ MIN

○ GOOD ○ RESTLESS ○ MIXED

energy ○ 1 ○ 2 ○ 3 ○ 4 ○ 5

mood ______________________

evening REFLECTION

DATE: ____________________ M T W Th F S S

morning GOALS & INTENTIONS

activity

STEPS:

health & nutrition

DON'T FORGET TO HYDRATE

BREAKFAST
SNACK
LUNCH
SNACK
DINNER

sleep ______ HRS ______ MIN

○ GOOD ○ RESTLESS ○ MIXED

energy ○ 1 ○ 2 ○ 3 ○ 4 ○ 5

mood ____________

evening REFLECTION

DATE: ______________ M T W Th F S S

morning GOALS & INTENTIONS

activity

STEPS:

health & nutrition

DON'T FORGET TO HYDRATE

BREAKFAST	
SNACK	
LUNCH	
SNACK	
DINNER	

sleep ______ HRS ______ MIN

○ GOOD ○ RESTLESS ○ MIXED

energy ○ 1 ○ 2 ○ 3 ○ 4 ○ 5

mood ______________

evening REFLECTION

DATE: ____________ M T W Th F S S

morning GOALS & INTENTIONS

activity

STEPS:

health & nutrition

DON'T FORGET TO HYDRATE

BREAKFAST	
SNACK	
LUNCH	
SNACK	
DINNER	

sleep ______ HRS ______ MIN

○ GOOD ○ RESTLESS ○ MIXED

energy ○ 1 ○ 2 ○ 3 ○ 4 ○ 5

mood ______

evening REFLECTION

DATE: ____________ M T W Th F S S

morning GOALS & INTENTIONS

activity

STEPS:

health & nutrition

DON'T FORGET TO HYDRATE

BREAKFAST	
SNACK	
LUNCH	
SNACK	
DINNER	

sleep ______ HRS ______ MIN

○ GOOD ○ RESTLESS ○ MIXED

energy ○ 1 ○ 2 ○ 3 ○ 4 ○ 5

mood ____________

evening REFLECTION

You don't grow to become who you were meant to be by sitting in one place. You become that person once you take a leap of faith.
Take a chance

Starting the morning with even 10 minutes of meditation sets you up for a day of intentional awareness and contentment. Close your eyes and clear your mind in a dark room or follow along with a guided meditation app. The benefits of meditation are well-documented and include reducing stress, increasing self-awareness and working toward being more present. If you find yourself getting antsy, start with just two minutes and add a minute each day. They call it the practice of meditation for a reason. There's no wrong way to do it, so keep practicing and get zen!

Measurements

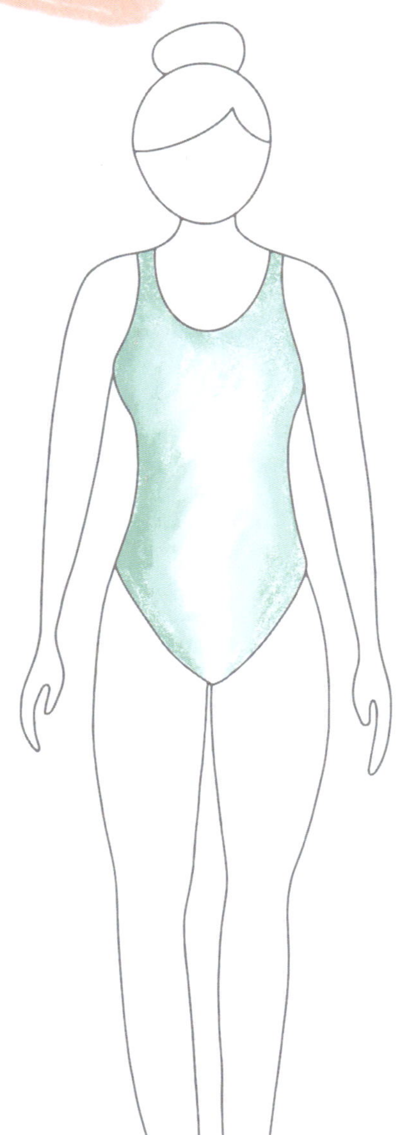

DATE: ____________________

UPPER ARM:

LEFT: ____________________

RIGHT: ____________________

CHEST: ____________________

WAIST: ____________________

HIPS: ____________________

LEGS:

LEFT: ____________________

RIGHT: ____________________

WEIGHT: ____________________

See page 10 for tips on getting accurate and consistent measurements!

Check-in time!

FITNESS

NUTRITION

GOALS

LIFESTYLE

WELLNESS

Reflection

DATE: ____________ M T W Th F S S

morning GOALS & INTENTIONS

activity

STEPS:

health & nutrition

DON'T FORGET TO HYDRATE

BREAKFAST

SNACK

LUNCH

SNACK

DINNER

sleep ______ HRS ______ MIN

○ GOOD ○ RESTLESS ○ MIXED

energy ○ 1 ○ 2 ○ 3 ○ 4 ○ 5

mood ____________

evening REFLECTION

DATE: ______________ M T W Th F S S

morning GOALS & INTENTIONS

activity

STEPS:

health & nutrition

DON'T FORGET TO HYDRATE

BREAKFAST	
SNACK	
LUNCH	
SNACK	
DINNER	

sleep ______ HRS ______ MIN

○ GOOD ○ RESTLESS ○ MIXED

energy ○ 1 ○ 2 ○ 3 ○ 4 ○ 5

mood ______

evening REFLECTION

DATE: ______________________ M T W Th F S S

morning GOALS & INTENTIONS

activity

STEPS:

health & nutrition

DON'T FORGET TO HYDRATE

BREAKFAST	
SNACK	
LUNCH	
SNACK	
DINNER	

sleep ________ HRS ________ MIN

○ GOOD ○ RESTLESS ○ MIXED

energy ○ 1 ○ 2 ○ 3 ○ 4 ○ 5

mood ______________________

evening REFLECTION

DATE: ____________ M T W Th F S S

morning GOALS & INTENTIONS

activity

STEPS:

health & nutrition

DON'T FORGET TO HYDRATE

BREAKFAST	
SNACK	
LUNCH	
SNACK	
DINNER	

sleep ______ HRS ______ MIN

○ GOOD ○ RESTLESS ○ MIXED

energy ○ 1 ○ 2 ○ 3 ○ 4 ○ 5

mood ____________

evening REFLECTION

DATE: ____________ M T W Th F S S

morning GOALS & INTENTIONS

activity

STEPS:

health & nutrition

DON'T FORGET TO HYDRATE

BREAKFAST	
SNACK	
LUNCH	
SNACK	
DINNER	

sleep ______ HRS ______ MIN

○ GOOD ○ RESTLESS ○ MIXED

energy ○ 1 ○ 2 ○ 3 ○ 4 ○ 5

mood ____________

evening REFLECTION

DATE: ______________ M T W Th F S S

morning GOALS & INTENTIONS

activity

STEPS:

health & nutrition

DON'T FORGET TO HYDRATE

BREAKFAST	
SNACK	
LUNCH	
SNACK	
DINNER	

sleep ______ HRS ______ MIN

○ GOOD ○ RESTLESS ○ MIXED

energy ○ 1 ○ 2 ○ 3 ○ 4 ○ 5

mood ______________

evening REFLECTION

DATE: ______________ M T W Th F S S

morning GOALS & INTENTIONS

activity

STEPS:

health & nutrition

DON'T FORGET TO HYDRATE

BREAKFAST	
SNACK	
LUNCH	
SNACK	
DINNER	

sleep ______ HRS ______ MIN

○ GOOD ○ RESTLESS ○ MIXED

energy ○ 1 ○ 2 ○ 3 ○ 4 ○ 5

mood ______________

evening REFLECTION

Comparison is the thief of joy

Theodore Roosevelt

The Importance of Self-Care

We live in a fast-paced society with mounting pressure to be the best, most productive version of ourselves. It's all too common to hear a busy adult state, "I haven't had a shower or proper meal in five days!" We are taught not to value self-care because being a good parent, partner, or employee means giving everything to everyone else and leaving nothing for ourselves. But remember that you can't pour from an empty cup. If you are not taking care of yourself, you aren't able to give the best version of yourself to anyone else either. Everyone deserves some time carved out for themselves. Take a walk without the kids. Book a massage. Prioritize that workout class you've been wanting to try. Do what you need to do in order to recharge and reset. And remember: a shower is not self-care! At the very least, play some music and fill the tub with bubbles.

DATE: ____________________ M T W Th F S S

morning GOALS & INTENTIONS

activity

STEPS:

health & nutrition

DON'T FORGET TO HYDRATE

BREAKFAST	
SNACK	
LUNCH	
SNACK	
DINNER	

sleep ______ HRS ______ MIN

○ GOOD ○ RESTLESS ○ MIXED

energy ○ 1 ○ 2 ○ 3 ○ 4 ○ 5

mood ____________________

evening REFLECTION

DATE: ____________________ M T W Th F S S

morning GOALS & INTENTIONS

activity

STEPS:

health & nutrition

DON'T FORGET TO HYDRATE

BREAKFAST	
SNACK	
LUNCH	
SNACK	
DINNER	

sleep ______ HRS ______ MIN

○ GOOD ○ RESTLESS ○ MIXED

energy ○ 1 ○ 2 ○ 3 ○ 4 ○ 5

mood ____________________

evening REFLECTION

DATE: ____________ M T W Th F S S

morning GOALS & INTENTIONS

activity

STEPS:

health & nutrition

DON'T FORGET TO HYDRATE

BREAKFAST	
SNACK	
LUNCH	
SNACK	
DINNER	

sleep ______ HRS ______ MIN

○ GOOD ○ RESTLESS ○ MIXED

energy ○ 1 ○ 2 ○ 3 ○ 4 ○ 5

mood ____________

evening REFLECTION

DATE: ____________________ M T W Th F S S

morning GOALS & INTENTIONS

____

____

____

____

activity

STEPS:

health & nutrition

DON'T FORGET TO HYDRATE

BREAKFAST	
SNACK	
LUNCH	
SNACK	
DINNER	

sleep ________ HRS ________ MIN

○ GOOD ○ RESTLESS ○ MIXED

energy ○ 1 ○ 2 ○ 3 ○ 4 ○ 5

mood ______________________

evening REFLECTION

____

____

____

____

DATE: ______________ M T W Th F S S

morning GOALS & INTENTIONS

activity

STEPS:

health & nutrition

DON'T FORGET TO HYDRATE

BREAKFAST	
SNACK	
LUNCH	
SNACK	
DINNER	

sleep ______ HRS ______ MIN

○ GOOD ○ RESTLESS ○ MIXED

energy ○ 1 ○ 2 ○ 3 ○ 4 ○ 5

mood ______________

evening REFLECTION

DATE: ______________ M T W Th F S S

morning GOALS & INTENTIONS

activity

STEPS:

health & nutrition

DON'T FORGET TO HYDRATE

BREAKFAST	
SNACK	
LUNCH	
SNACK	
DINNER	

sleep ______ HRS ______ MIN

○ GOOD ○ RESTLESS ○ MIXED

energy ○ 1 ○ 2 ○ 3 ○ 4 ○ 5

mood ______________

evening REFLECTION

DATE: ______________ M T W Th F S S

morning GOALS & INTENTIONS

activity

STEPS:

health & nutrition

DON'T FORGET TO HYDRATE

BREAKFAST	
SNACK	
LUNCH	
SNACK	
DINNER	

sleep ______ HRS ______ MIN

○ GOOD ○ RESTLESS ○ MIXED

energy ○ 1 ○ 2 ○ 3 ○ 4 ○ 5

mood ______________

evening REFLECTION

With work, family, appointments, and responsibilities, it can feel like there is no time to stop and smell the coffee, not to mention the roses! The art of practicing gratitude involves taking a few short moments each day to reflect on our life and treasure the moments that make the day sparkle. The big ones (a promotion! Hitting a fitness milestone! Spending time with a loved one!) may be obvious, but finding gratitude in the small, quiet moments is just as important.

Maybe you snuck in 15 minutes of yoga between calls and errands. Maybe you finished that load of laundry that's been taunting you for a week. Or maybe it's as simple as a warm mug of your favorite chai tea. Keeping a gratitude journal or a small notebook to jot down a few things you are grateful for before bed is linked to a number of positive benefits. When you go to bed having reflected on all the good things you have in life, it fills you with positivity and love. In that moment, the hard seems less hard and the positive stuff, the moments you're grateful for, is what gives you the peace to fall asleep with a full and happy heart.

DATE: ______________ M T W Th F S S

morning GOALS & INTENTIONS

activity

STEPS:

health & nutrition

DON'T FORGET TO HYDRATE

BREAKFAST	
SNACK	
LUNCH	
SNACK	
DINNER	

sleep ______ HRS ______ MIN

○ GOOD ○ RESTLESS ○ MIXED

energy ○ 1 ○ 2 ○ 3 ○ 4 ○ 5

mood ______________

evening REFLECTION

DATE: ____________________ M T W Th F S S

morning GOALS & INTENTIONS

activity

STEPS:

health & nutrition

DON'T FORGET TO HYDRATE

BREAKFAST	
SNACK	
LUNCH	
SNACK	
DINNER	

sleep ______ HRS ______ MIN

○ GOOD ○ RESTLESS ○ MIXED

energy ○ 1 ○ 2 ○ 3 ○ 4 ○ 5

mood ____________

evening REFLECTION

DATE: ______________________ M T W Th F S S

morning GOALS & INTENTIONS

activity

STEPS:

health & nutrition

DON'T FORGET TO HYDRATE

BREAKFAST	
SNACK	
LUNCH	
SNACK	
DINNER	

sleep ______ HRS ______ MIN

○ GOOD ○ RESTLESS ○ MIXED

energy ○ 1 ○ 2 ○ 3 ○ 4 ○ 5

mood ______________________

evening REFLECTION

DATE: ______________________ M T W Th F S S

morning GOALS & INTENTIONS

activity

STEPS:

health & nutrition

DON'T FORGET TO HYDRATE

BREAKFAST	
SNACK	
LUNCH	
SNACK	
DINNER	

sleep ________ HRS ________ MIN

○ GOOD ○ RESTLESS ○ MIXED

energy ○ 1 ○ 2 ○ 3 ○ 4 ○ 5

mood ____________________

evening REFLECTION

DATE: ______________________ M T W Th F S S

morning GOALS & INTENTIONS

activity

STEPS:

health & nutrition

DON'T FORGET TO HYDRATE

BREAKFAST	
SNACK	
LUNCH	
SNACK	
DINNER	

sleep ________ HRS ________ MIN

○ GOOD ○ RESTLESS ○ MIXED

energy ○ 1 ○ 2 ○ 3 ○ 4 ○ 5

mood ______________________

evening REFLECTION

DATE: ____________ M T W Th F S S

morning GOALS & INTENTIONS

______

______

______

______

activity

STEPS:

health & nutrition

DON'T FORGET TO HYDRATE

BREAKFAST	
SNACK	
LUNCH	
SNACK	
DINNER	

sleep ______ HRS ______ MIN

○ GOOD ○ RESTLESS ○ MIXED

energy ○ 1 ○ 2 ○ 3 ○ 4 ○ 5

mood ______

evening REFLECTION

______

______

______

 ______

DATE: ______________ M T W Th F S S

morning GOALS & INTENTIONS

activity

STEPS:

health & nutrition

DON'T FORGET TO HYDRATE

BREAKFAST	
SNACK	
LUNCH	
SNACK	
DINNER	

sleep ______ HRS ______ MIN

○ GOOD ○ RESTLESS ○ MIXED

energy ○ 1 ○ 2 ○ 3 ○ 4 ○ 5

mood ______________

evening REFLECTION

Picture this: you are working hard, establishing healthy fitness and eating habits, and you show up to your Uncle Bill's 60th birthday party where they are serving your favorite red velvet cake with extra cream cheese frosting. It is okay to sometimes have the cake! Life is too short to only eat kale. But pay attention to how your body and mind feel after eating certain foods. You may find that you have more energy when you incorporate more vegetables, lean proteins, and whole grains. Fuel your body, eat whole foods, but treat yourself. It is also important to remember to eat mindfully. Lounging in front of the TV with a bag of potato chips often leads to overindulging and feeling guilty. Whether you are having a fresh spinach salad or Uncle Bill's red velvet cake, take the time to appreciate your food, how it tastes, and how it is nourishing your body.

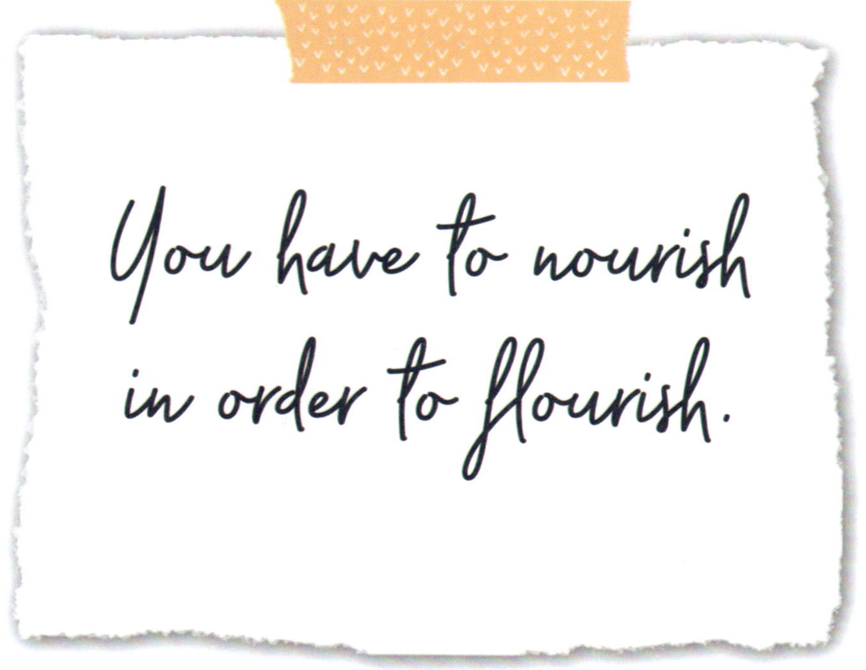

DATE: ____________ M T W Th F S S

morning GOALS & INTENTIONS

activity

STEPS:

health & nutrition

DON'T FORGET TO HYDRATE

BREAKFAST	
SNACK	
LUNCH	
SNACK	
DINNER	

sleep ______ HRS ______ MIN

○ GOOD ○ RESTLESS ○ MIXED

energy ○ 1 ○ 2 ○ 3 ○ 4 ○ 5

mood ____________

evening REFLECTION

DATE: ____________ M T W Th F S S

morning GOALS & INTENTIONS

activity

STEPS:

health & nutrition

DON'T FORGET TO HYDRATE

BREAKFAST	
SNACK	
LUNCH	
SNACK	
DINNER	

sleep ______ HRS ______ MIN

○ GOOD ○ RESTLESS ○ MIXED

energy ○ 1 ○ 2 ○ 3 ○ 4 ○ 5

mood ____________

evening REFLECTION

DATE: ____________________ M T W Th F S S

morning GOALS & INTENTIONS

activity

STEPS:

health & nutrition

DON'T FORGET TO HYDRATE

BREAKFAST	
SNACK	
LUNCH	
SNACK	
DINNER	

sleep ________ HRS ________ MIN

○ GOOD ○ RESTLESS ○ MIXED

energy ○ 1 ○ 2 ○ 3 ○ 4 ○ 5

mood ____________________

evening REFLECTION

DATE: ______________________ M T W Th F S S

morning GOALS & INTENTIONS

activity

STEPS:

health & nutrition

DON'T FORGET TO HYDRATE

BREAKFAST	
SNACK	
LUNCH	
SNACK	
DINNER	

sleep ________ HRS ________ MIN

○ GOOD ○ RESTLESS ○ MIXED

energy ○ 1 ○ 2 ○ 3 ○ 4 ○ 5

mood ______________________

evening REFLECTION

DATE: ______________ M T W Th F S S

morning GOALS & INTENTIONS

____

____

____

____

activity

STEPS:

health & nutrition

DON'T FORGET TO HYDRATE

BREAKFAST	
SNACK	
LUNCH	
SNACK	
DINNER	

sleep ______ HRS ______ MIN

○ GOOD ○ RESTLESS ○ MIXED

energy ○ 1 ○ 2 ○ 3 ○ 4 ○ 5

mood ______________

evening REFLECTION

____

____

____

____

DATE: ______________ M T W Th F S S

morning GOALS & INTENTIONS

activity

STEPS:

health & nutrition

DON'T FORGET TO HYDRATE

BREAKFAST	
SNACK	
LUNCH	
SNACK	
DINNER	

sleep ______ HRS ______ MIN

○ GOOD ○ RESTLESS ○ MIXED

energy ○ 1 ○ 2 ○ 3 ○ 4 ○ 5

mood ______

evening REFLECTION

DATE: ______________ M T W Th F S S

morning GOALS & INTENTIONS

activity

STEPS:

health & nutrition

DON'T FORGET TO HYDRATE

BREAKFAST	
SNACK	
LUNCH	
SNACK	
DINNER	

sleep ______ HRS ______ MIN

○ GOOD ○ RESTLESS ○ MIXED

energy ○ 1 ○ 2 ○ 3 ○ 4 ○ 5

mood ______________

evening REFLECTION

CONGRATS!

Health is a Lifestyle

NOT A 30-DAY CHALLENGE

Check-in time!

FITNESS

NUTRITION

GOALS

LIFESTYLE

WELLNESS

Measurements

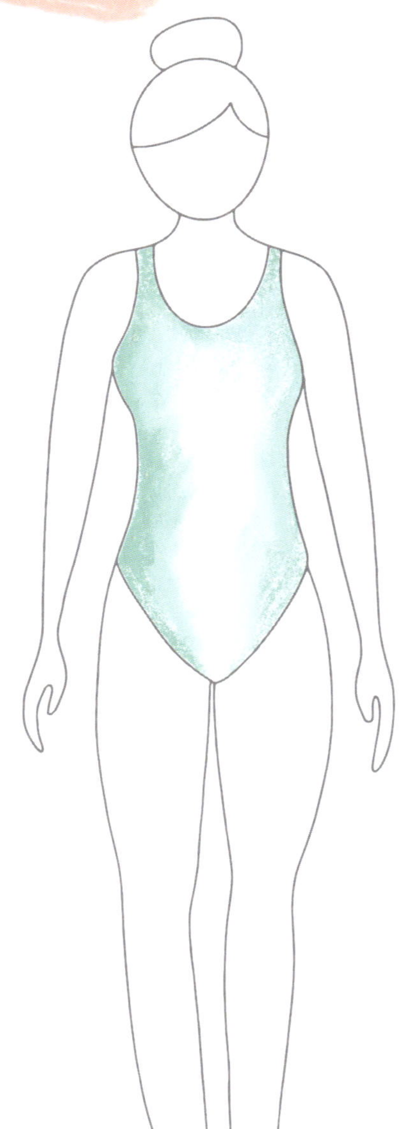

DATE: ____________________

UPPER ARM:

LEFT: ____________________

RIGHT: ____________________

CHEST: ____________________

WAIST: ____________________

HIPS: ____________________

LEGS:

LEFT: ____________________

RIGHT: ____________________

WEIGHT: ____________________

See page 10 for tips on getting accurate and consistent measurements!

Reflection

what now?

First and foremost, give yourself the biggest pat on the back, because you committed to this fitness planner and YOU DID IT! It doesn't matter if every day was a perfect day, or that maybe you stopped for a while and then started back up again. What matters is that you showed up for yourself and your health. Remember that progress is made over time, not just in a matter of days or weeks. It is so important that you keep going and gaining momentum. Take what you have learned from this journal and use it going forward.

As you continue on your fitness journey, make sure you don't get too comfortable in your bubble and hit a plateau. Switch things up, try a new fitness program with new goals, increase your weights or set a new running goal. You have set an amazing foundation, so now is the time to build on it.

On the nutrition front, listen to what your body has taught you from this prcoess. You have the basis for healthy eating so continue to experiment with new recipes and ingredients. Maybe you want to try going 30 days without processed sugar or incorporating a green vegetable with every meal. Have fun with food and always be mindful of how it is fueling your body.

You have set the habits whether you are conscious of it or not, so continue to thrive in this new lifestyle you have created for yourself. Congratulations! You are amazing!

FITNESS:

LIFESTYLE:

NUTRITION:

WELLNESS:

Notes

Notes

Notes

Notes

Notes

Notes